If These Trees Could Talk, Park 1
Stories from the Trees of Sunset Park

Kate Trnka

Sacred Earth Publishing
A Division of ALTERNATIVES Holistic Health & Wellness Center, LLC
2014

If These Trees Could Talk, Park 1:
Stories of the Trees of Sunset Park

First Edition – April 8, 2014

Written by: Kate Trnka
Photography by: Kate Trnka
Publisher: Sacred Earth Publishing
(A Division of ALTERNATIVES Holistic Health & Wellness Center, LLC)

All rights reserved. No part of this book may be reproduced or transmitted in any form by any means without written permission from the author. The author of this book does not dispense medical advice or prescribe the use of any technique as a form of treatment for any physical, emotional, or medical problems without the advice of a physician – either directly or indirectly. The intent of the author is only to offer information of a personal nature to help you in your quest for emotional and spiritual well-being. In the event you use any of the information in this book for yourself, the author assumes no responsibility for your actions.

ISBN: 978-0-9960979-0-1

For more information, visit the author's website:
www.SacredEarthWellness.net or www.AlternativesHolisticHealth.com

April, 2014
Printed in the United States of America

Table of Contents

Dedication	i
Acknowledgements	ii
Preface	iii
Prologue	v
Gaia	1
The Sentinels	5
Randy	8
Geo, Isis, Jiminy	12
Isis	16
Singer	21
The Medicine Man	24
Adam	27
Gandau	30
Merci	34
Cheyenne	37
Harley	40
Treo	42
The Eagle Tree	45
Scotty	48
Iglemisus	51
Persephone	54
Aires	57
Sarah	60
Arthur	63
Audrey	66
Abigail	68
Jeremy	71
Geronimo	73
Liberty	75
Paz	77
The Angel Tree	79
Harley (again)	82
Rose/Bella/Bertha	84
Edward	87
Epilogue	89

DEDICATION

I dedicate this book to Creator – who made this world ONE. To Creator, who made this world work so miraculously and so beautifully. To Creator who inspires me each and every day to make right choices. To Creator who through Hir works of beauty helped me to recognize the interconnectedness of ALL that is, and how, through our actions, we DO make a difference – one way or another.

ACKNOWLEDGEMENTS

First of all I want to thank my parents for bringing me to life. Mom, you were the person who showed me that every THING does have a soul, thank you. The person who's tough love also showed me the grace of God. Dad, thanks for inspiring me to finish it!

Thank you to Carol Bridges and Lorrie Collins for teaching me how to communicate with nature. Thanks to the goddesses of Wild Grace whose wisdom, support and love have encouraged me for all of these years. And to my family and friends, I give you my thanks and appreciation for supporting me even when my thoughts and actions seemed a little "out there".

But, most of all I want to thank Creator and all the "Standing People" for showing me once again, how to listen.

PREFACE

"Pick me! Pick me!"

"I've got a story for you!"

"So do I!"

This is what I heard one fall day as I set out to the woods looking for a particular tree I had discovered a few days earlier. So, here are a few of the stories I've captured from these willing participants. I have this strange feeling that this is only the beginning...for you, for me, and for the Standing People!

I don't pretend to know too much about trees – from a scientific standpoint anyway. But I do know about my experiences with them and I want to share them with you. Yes, I talk to trees. Yes, I hug trees. Yes, I believe that trees have spirits and that they can communicate with us. I hope that by the time I finish these stories that I have a deeper knowledge and understanding of trees and I hope that by sharing these stories with you that you too develop a deeper understanding and appreciation for the "Standing People".

Trees don't communicate with voices that can be heard by the human ear, as we are accustomed to hearing. But they do have something to say and we can *listen* to them. After all, hearing and listening are two different skills. To hear is to perceive sound by the ear, while to listen is to pay attention; to try to hear. I believe trees, and all of nature, communicate the way Creator had designed us to communicate – with no articulated words. Call it telepathy if you like. I believe the fall of man came when we forgot, or chose not to (free will), communicate (listen) in this fashion. By not listening we became separated from God. By the way, I will use the word *God* in my writings to refer to that mysterious force that is beyond our reasoning and imaginations, the One who created all that is; the One who knows us and lives within us – (and if you don't know this now, I hope you come to know it) – the One that lives within ALL things.

But, please don't let the word "God" conjure up any long-held negative feelings about religion, because these stories have nothing to do with religion, rather they have to do with "knowing." *Knowing* that the Universe we live in is greater than anything we can imagine! *Knowing* that we get to be a part of it. *Knowing* that each of us has a role to play. *Knowing* that we are all interconnected. *Knowing* that each choice we make impacts the world we live in. *Knowing* that driving nails into a tree will injure it and may even kill it. I have seen this. (See "Randy and the Dying Ones.") *Knowing* that it starts and ends with every choice we make. And one of those choices is whether or not we choose to listen. I have chosen to listen to the stories of the trees. I have chosen to share them with you.

I may use the term hir from time to time when the gender of the trees' spirit was not made known to me (or if I forgot to, or when it didn't seem important to differentiate its gender). I wanted to know the trees I wrote about – know hir name, know hir "tribe", and of course know hir story.

Please note that the first couple of "visits" with these trees (Gaia, The Sentinels, Randy), were only to be part of my journal – my personal experiences, therefore their messages aren't as defined as later messages. Still, I believe these stories set the stage for the intimate relationships one can have with nature. Anyway, when the messages seemed to be more messages of a universal nature (Beginning with Isis) – and there were so many of them – I felt compelled to share them with you. Please don't view these words as my words, but read these words with the understanding that these were messages I needed to hear. The reason I'm sharing them with you is so that you may know that it is possible to find your answers in nature and that maybe these words will have meaning for you, at any given moment as well.

Now, I invite you into the woods with me so you can know their stories, too.

Come along – I have lots of interesting "people" for you to meet!

PROLOGUE
Kids and Trees

One day, a gorgeous late fall day, instead of having class indoors, I decided to take my first grade classes out for a walk while our classrooms were being used for other purposes. There was a set of woods adjacent to the school where I taught and they were drawing me over to spend time there. So, when the children arrived that day I told them that we were going to walk over to some friends' house. Well, I admitted it wasn't exactly a house as far as houses go, but we would definitely be visitors and as such, should be respectful on our visit. So we got together in small groups, attached ourselves to small ropes and walked onward.

When we got to the edge of the woods, I told the children that we were going in there - as I pointed to the woods. They were all excited - they started walking toward the woods. But, before they got too far, I asked them if they had asked permission to enter. They said they hadn't. The rest of the story goes something like this:

"Well, if you were going over to someone's house, would you just go in, or would you knock on the door or ring the door bell?"
"We'd knock first," everyone chimed in.

So I explained, "We can't exactly knock on a door, but there is a door of sorts into these woods. I think we should ask the trees if it's okay to come in."
The kids all started asking, *"Can we come in?"*
"Can we come in?"

I stopped them and suggested that they stop being verbal and instead, ask in their minds and hearts that same question - silently. That's how much of nature communicates... in silence. So the kids paused and we all stood silent for a moment in time. Then I asked, "Did anyone get an answer?" And every single child either said, *"Yes."* Or, *"It's okay to go in."* Or, *"They said it was okay."*
So, into the woods we traveled.

During the first trip into the woods that day (with my first class), I merely told the children simple things, or asked simple questions like, "Did you know that the bigger the tree is, the older it is?"

"If we're quiet we might see some creatures in the woods."
I was so amused at the excitement when a student would catch a glimpse of a squirrel.

But little did we know what special gift we were about to receive - the sight of a red-tailed hawk in a tree bordering the back edge of the woods. I stood still and turned to the students with my finger placed in front of my pursed lips ... and pointed to the tree where the hawk stood and whispered, "Look in the tree. There's a hawk."

It seems only the first couple of groups were able to catch a glimpse of him before he flew into a nearby tree still within my view. He seemed to be as curious about us as we were of him. He stayed there looking at us, and us looking at him, until we decided to move on.

We walked on - pointing at things and enjoying the beautiful day. Once we got to the other side of the woods (before it was time to turn around and head back) I asked the kids if they had ever hugged a tree. No one had. They looked at me kind of funny when I said, "Trees love hugs ... just like people do. I hug trees all the time."

I told them, that if they wanted to, I'd give them two minutes to try and hug 6 trees and be back here to meet up with the group. The kids loved it! I could see it in their faces. Such delight!

It was time to return to school. We had gotten in a terrific class and even had some light exercise in the process. It felt like light exercise to me, but I guess the walk was plenty for these young ones!

The next class (I had five classes on this particular day) started out similarly although we didn't have the good fortune to see the hawk. However, this time when we got to the edge of the woods, and I started telling them about hugging trees, I decided to take it a bit further. I told the students that I thank the trees when I give them a hug. I decided to show them what I did. When I got to the tree, I hugged it and said something like this, "Thank you so much for your beauty, for the shade you provide to people and animals. Thank you for your life and helping us to breathe better. Thanks for the pretty leaves and giving protection to all of the animals."

Then, I asked the kids if they wanted to hug the trees, and if they wanted to, they could say something to the trees, too. All of them did. I gave them 2 minutes to hug and talk to at least three trees. When they returned back to the group circle, I asked them if they would like to share what they had said to the trees. I got many responses. Most of them,
"I told my tree, 'Thank you'."
"I love you."
"Thank you for your shade."

The next two classes went something like the first two, but building upon the experience of the first two classes. During the last class, once we got to our circle at the other side of the woods, it went something like this...
I talked about how I hugged the trees and thanked them for their life. Then, I asked the students if they wanted to hug and talk to the trees.

"Yeah!!"

I told them I'd give them two minutes to "hang out" with a tree and then to meet back here.
When we all gathered back together, I asked, "Who said something to their tree?" Everyone raised their hand.
"What did you say?" I had similar responses as in previous classes.

"I love you."
"Thanks."

Then I asked, "Did anyone's tree talk back to you?" At first, my question was met with silence. Then, I heard a couple of students say, "NOoooooo!" followed by mocking laughter. But one brave little girl said, *"Mine did!"*

So, I asked her, "What did it say?"

She said it had said, *"I love you, too."*

All of a sudden, everyone was brave enough to share their conversational experience with their tree!
We went around the circle with those who wanted to share. Then I started back at the beginning and asked the first little girl, "Could you tell what kind of tree it was? I mean, was it a mama tree, or a papa tree, or a grandma tree, or a grandpa tree, or a little kid tree?"
She said, *"It was a woman tree."*

We went around the circle again to ask if the kids could tell me the gender and age of the tree. I thought that perhaps the boys would say they had spoken with a boy tree and the girls with a girl tree. But, it did not turn out that way at all. There were trees of both genders and of all ages! The kids were excited to share and I was so amazed by how they were so naturally tuned into the trees' spirits.

On the way out of the woods, this last time, one little girl was skipping through the woods, waving and saying out loud, *"Hi grandpa! Hi sister! Hi friend!"* And on and on she went!

Each time we left the woods, we thanked our hosts ... and we left the door... open!

I wanted to share this story with you, because it made me so very aware of how far away we can get from opening our hearts to all that is. Most adults would scoff at talking with trees, but it felt so very natural to these little folks. I believe that if we approached the world with a child's heart we would have a better understanding of how we should communicate, how we should treat things, and how we should love. I believe that as adults we have a lot to learn from nature, from each other and... from our children.

GAIA

"Believe one who knows: you will find something greater in woods than in books. Trees and stones will teach you that which you can never learn from masters." - St. Bernard

GAIA

My first *tree experience* was with Gaia – I had been walking through the woods one crisp fall day, a few years ago. She caught my attention. She was so large and strong and beautiful. As I approached her a profound love swept over me, along with a deep sense of grief for the pain that had been issued to her.

Many, many folks had carved their initials into her body. Some had driven railroad pegs into her. Many nails had been driven into her. I went home to get my hammer. I was saddened each time I removed a nail and placed my hand over the injured area. I got all of the nails out, but one. I tried to remove it – I tried and tried ... until my hammer broke in two. It was then that I figured out it was to stay as a symbol to others (and to me) of her courage and strength.

The railroad peg is to be a part of her forever. Her inner strength has allowed her to live despite the penetration of this foreign material. We both began reliving the past hurts – hers and mine - both of us recognizing that we have overcome many adversities. I came to realize that it is through overcoming these adversities that I have gained strength, and more importantly, wisdom.

It was then that I realized how wise Gaia really was. She had been here for a very long time, much longer than I. It was then that I knew she was to be my teacher. I greet Gaia each time I enter the woods now and sometimes I stop for a visit and other times we just say hello.*

But I do want to share this message that she gave to me one day, for it forever changed my life.

"I speak with the wisdom of the ages...
The leaves all around your feet... and mine...Are symbols reflecting the changing times
My passion runs strongly like the river at its best
Tumbling, crashing, billowing over rock after rock
My passion for you ... for life... is like this ...

(* Gaia is no longer strong and vibrant. She is transitioning from one of the Standing People to one of the Fallen Ones.)

*And yet, at times and places, it's gentler
As the river caresses the roots of the trees that grow nearby and the leaves
drop in to fertilize the soil which lies beneath
as it caresses and smoothes the rocks' hard surfaces
just as my love for you
has softened my very heart and soul*

*Twisting, turning, bending
Flowing where there are no barriers;
Just as there are no barriers
When my soul reaches toward yours*

*Sometimes debris gets in the way – leaves and branches
And we get stuck
We always find our way around things*

In this world you will become what you seek

*Your roots grow deep and people will feed off you – let them
That is why you are here–
protect yourself though
There are those who seek to harm you and those like you*

*People's souls are ready for the harvest. Seeds have been planted
By those who have come and gone before you –
Even you have planted a seed many lives ago
The time is now… to gather the harvest
And to sow many seeds*

There is much to do
Your path is genuine
Go now and fulfill your desires
Because they are mine too.

Those that know not – see me not
You will know who I am ... I will give you a sign.

Little did I know how her words would affect me. Little did I know who she really was. I still know little, yet it is my passion to learn more about her and as you will soon learn, what she had in store for me.

THE SENTINELS

"The tree which moves some to tears of joy is in the eyes of others only a green thing which stands in the way. Some see Nature all ridicule and deformity, and by these I shall not regulate my proportions; and some scarce see Nature at all. But to the eyes of the man of imagination, Nature is Imagination itself. As a man, so he sees." - William Blake

THE SENTINELS

Do you know how you can be someplace over and over and over and again and not notice something and then the next time you go there, something really sticks out? You wonder how long it's been there and why you didn't notice it before? When that has happened to me, I've come to the conclusion that perhaps, I wasn't ready to notice it. Perhaps I wasn't open to noticing it. Perhaps I wasn't meant to notice it – not until that time when I did.

This is how it was with "The Sentinels." There I was on my morning jog – on the path I had taken time and time again. And all of I a sudden I hear, "*Halt!*" I stopped and looked up at this big, and I mean BIG tree.

It seemed familiar to me in some vague way. So, I stopped and said hello and as I did this I recognized him from long before. I said to him, finally with recognition, "It's so nice to see you again"– he allowed me to give him a hug and he patronizingly and awkwardly gave me a hug back and patted me on the back. He quickly said, *"It's good to see you too, but there is someone who has been wanting to see you for quite some time"* as he gestured over to his right, my left. I quickly wheeled around and without words, saw my long-lost friend. I can't explain to you how I knew this "person", but I knew hir and I knew hir well. (Hir is a term I will use from time to time when gender is not important or not recognized or when the individual transcends gender boundaries. It could be a him or a her, but it really doesn't matter.)

It was as if we were twins, separated by some unseen and unexpected force and now we were reunited again. I held hir in my arms for minutes and minutes, feeling the tears of joy beginning to flow; for we had finally joined again, in spirit, with one another. It seemed like lifetimes ago when we had last been together – and indeed it had been. Words were not exchanged, we just conveyed our love for one another in that language that is beyond words – the language that can be spoken and heard without forming words – the language that was before language as we know it today.

After our reunion, I looked at these two "Sentinels" (that is what I call them) because each of them stood on opposite sides of the path where I go walking/jogging. Their duty seemed to be to guard something. Perhaps one day I will know more of their story and what it is they are guarding, but for now I only know that I found a long-lost friend and I'm grateful to hir brother for causing me to stop, slow down and take notice!!

RANDY

"May my life be like a great hospitable tree,
and may weary wanderers find in me a rest."
- John Henry Jowett

Randy and the Dying Ones

Why do we do what we do?! How can man not see how interconnected with nature we really are?

I was jogging through the woods this morning, but when I came upon Gaia, I decided to pay her a visit. It is always so refreshing to my soul to talk with her. She always seems to teach me a lesson. She said, "*Look around. There are other trees and other lessons to be learned.*"

I looked around and saw the majesty of the wooded area I have come to love and am only just beginning to know. I resumed jogging, but quickly saw another tree that attracted my attention. I made my way toward it.

Once I arrived I realized how magnificent it really was. It must be very old, but as I write this I'm not knowledgeable enough to know how old it is. But, just to give you an idea it would take three adults to be able to put our arms around it.

He said, "*My name is Randy.*"
"Randy"? (I was thinking he'd have this unique and majestic name).
"*Well, it's Randolph actually.*" (I laughed)

I looked at Randy and began to realize that the very trees that attracted me, have attracted other humans before me, for Randy had a wood plank between two of his branches. Someone had spent some time with Randy and apparently lots of it. I went on.

I began jogging again, and as I was headed up the hill, instead of focusing on the task at hand (making it up the hill without having to stop), I began looking at the trees. One in particular stood out, perhaps due to its size or perhaps the number of trunks that sprung from it - three. It wasn't that far in and after asking permission to come visit from the other trees, I entered to meet it (so much for my cardio workout). Anyway, as I approached this old friend, it was filled with moss and some mushrooms were growing on its trunk. It didn't take me too long to conclude that this tree was dying. I was immediately saddened - thanking it for its life, for its lessons, for everything it had given the earth. I reminded hir that its remnants would remain for a long time and become a habitat for many and continue to recycle itself until it was of the earth.

In my "infinite wisdom" I warned the other nearby trees and felt saddened that they may meet their own death when this one fell. And they told me, "*This is our purpose. We are here to support the fall of this Great One.*"

It was why they were here? Can you believe that? What a wonderful lesson!! Thank you all of you young one's! And they say we can't learn from our youth! I was humbled once again – as I often am in nature.

I began to look for a way out, so as not to step on any young shoots. While doing this I noticed another large tree with a felled a branch. I was able to identify this tree as an oak as it still had two leaves clinging to it (it's the middle of December in Wisconsin). I believe it would take two adults, maybe two-and-a-half to get their arms around this one. Anyway, I wondered why this tree had lost this branch and noticed that just above the loss was a rope attached to a nail that had been driven into the tree. I shook my head, not wanting to believe that this was the cause of the amputation.

I walked around the tree and on the other side an even greater limb had fallen off. The trunk was beginning to rot out from within. I was shocked and at first I attributed it to having been struck by lightning. I held the limb and was full of grief. While holding it I was struck by something I saw within the trunk – some sap had frozen into a stalactite. The tree seemed to be weeping the loss as well. I looked closely at the fallen limb and noticed a nail on what would have been the outside of the tree. I pulled it out (as if that was going to make a difference – I think I just wanted it to). Then I noticed another, and another and another. I quit looking. But then I looked at the same limb, but from what would have been within the tree and I could see the butt end of a number of nails. I looked back on the outer side, but could not see the heads of these nails. The tree had absorbed these nails within itself over time, and as a result was killed by these nails. Some nails were still in the part of the tree that remained standing - just above and to the side of where the large limb had fallen off.

I went back to the other limb, looked at the rope that had been driven into the tree, and knew that was why this limb had fallen as well. I shook my head and left the woods. I jogged the rest of the way home. I wondered if the person(s) who drove these nails knew that this would be the end result, and very quickly realized that we all do "dumb" things, but usually it's because we don't think (obviously). And it's usually because we are either in a hurry, or suffering from a bout of greed.
So it was upon this experience that I began to write down my tree stories. Just as I have learned from the trees, I hope too, that you will learn from them as well.

Randy and the Sitting Place

Isis, Jiminy and Geoffrey ("Geo")

Isis   Jiminy

"What did the tree learn from the earth
to be able to talk with the sky?"
- Pablo Neruda

Today I met Isis and Jiminy and Geoffrey (also known as "Geo").

I set out to find out the names of the two dying trees that I had met on an earlier visit, not knowing what my experience would be today (one never knows). I know that if my heart is open, that I will experience just what I need to experience. It is when I am too hurried or when I begin to ignore, that I get "tripped up" in life.

Well, anyway, I was on my way to see the Dying One's ... but on the way I came across a tree which caught my attention. It was a large shaggy bark hickory tree – I loved the way its bark seemed to be peeling right off of it yet was firmly attached. It was surrounded by several smaller trees or bushes (2-3 feet tall). I carefully made my way to the standing one and held it near my heart, as I always do, sending it love. I knew that my heart wasn't as open as it needed to be, so I stood there for quite some time until my heart opened to the tree. It was then that I learned its name, Isis.

Well, Isis really didn't have too much to say today, her story will come at another time. But I did learn that the trees that surrounded her were there for protection, camouflage, if you will. And they did just that. I have ran or walked by Isis on numerous occasions, noticing her but never *really* noticing her and I KNOW it was because of those smaller trees. In this case that is a wonderful thing, for Isis stands alone, not surrounded by several other larger trees. I believe that if she were exposed that someone may have started carving into her, so I was grateful for the role these other little one's were playing. I moved away from Isis, careful not to damage the smaller ones and on the way out noticed another hickory tree, bent over but somehow still standing very tall. I knew that this tree had a message for me. But first, I stood back to look at Isis and told her I'd be back to learn of her story.

I approached the bent hickory and held it in my arms and quickly I heard it speak to me. After the initial "hellos" and "I love you's", it told me, *"Do not forget why you are here. You must continue on your path - the path that was chosen for you."*
"Thank you," I said and I asked it for its name.
"I am the voice of your conscience," he said. *"I know I remind you of someone else so you may call me that."* ... So, guess what I called him? Jiminy! I knew that I had received what I was to receive from Jiminy (at least for today) so onward I went to find the Dying One's.

I felt lost ... I was trying to find some old friends and yet I could not. I did find one of them. The other is near there, but I will have to wait for another time as the wind was biting through my jeans, my face was left exposed to the chill of the winter wind. But I did find one of the Dying One's. I spend a brief amount of time with him. "I am Geo – short for Geoffrey. But my friends call me Geo." I sat in his broken body, where one of the branches had peeled away and felt very close to this huge old oak tree. Geo was not "bleeding" today like he had been that day – that day when I wept for the loss of his life. He seemed content today. He made me feel that same way as I sat, welcomed, on his tortured body. He told me to go home and get warm, that he would see me again. And so I did. And, so I will.

Geo and his broken limbs

"Hurt not ... the trees."

Revelation 7:3

Geo and broken limb

Geo and the spike

Geo and the nails

ISIS

"We must protect the forests for our children, grandchildren and children yet to be born. We must protect the forests for those who can't speak for themselves such as the birds, animals, fish and trees."

- Chief Edward Moody, Qwatsinas, Nuxalk Nation

ISIS: The Storyteller

I spent some time with Isis today ... Isis is the Standing One that is surrounded by a circle of little trees, who are there to keep her protected. I quickly found out that Isis loves to tell stories. Today she told me a story she heard from her grandmother. It was after hearing this story that I knew I had to share this, and subsequently, future stories with you.

This is the story she told me:
"Once a long, long time ago there lived people on this land. They were peaceful people – people who loved the earth. They loved the birds and the other animals. They hunted and fished, but always honored those that gave up their lives so that the people could eat."

(Then she allowed me to see the story as she was telling it.)
I saw two men paddling into the river's cove with a birch-bark canoe, while the children ran to see what they had brought back from the trade. I saw the women who dropped their baskets near the creek so they could greet their returning loved ones. I saw the children, playing in the woods – some pretending to be warriors – some following fox tracks – some imitating the squirrels that were frolicking in the trees.

Some of the older girls were down near the creek, helping their mothers and grandmothers with the tasks at hand. While some of the boys had made spears, trying to bring in some fresh fish for the evening meal. The cawing of the crow was heard from a nearby tree and later it could be heard from a distant tree - still cawing, letting the people know of its presence. Everyone seemed so happy! I was given the ability to catch just a glimpse of the lives of the people that lived there.

I said to Isis, "It would have been so wonderful to have been a part of it – it seemed so genuine, so natural ... so peaceful."

"*Indeed, it was!*" She told me. "*But then ...*" she paused for what seemed like such a long time.

"But, what?" I asked. I sensed her sadness as she went on...

"Then it all changed. The white man came - the ones that the people had heard so much about. The ones that caused many tribes like theirs to have to leave their homelands or be killed. Although some knew this might eventually happen someday – it was hard for them to comprehend it happening to them in this wonderful and peaceful place. Arguments started to take place even amongst the people of the land as to how they were going to handle things when the white man came with their weapons. Some wanted to try and fight them off. Some wanted to pack up and leave. There were many arguments... many. The people were divided."

I interrupted, and asked, "Isis?"

"*Yes, dear?*" she answered.

"I once found myself at a place in the park that seemed as if at one time it may have been a sacred circle."

"Yes?"

"And I was drawn to walk toward a certain section of the woods." I showed Isis in my mind's eye where I was. (It was in a place not too far from where the dying one's stood.)

She acknowledged me, knowing the place I was referring to.

"Is this the place where many people lost their lives?" I asked.

"Yes," she said. *"But not for the reason that you think. But that is best left for another to tell you that story – someone who was closer to the situation than my grandmother. My grandmother knew of the story, but would never speak of it."*

"I understand," I said. I knew I would try and find a Standing Person who was willing to share that story with me another time. But for now, I had more questions.

"How did things look before the streets and sidewalks were here? How did it look on top of the hill where the ball diamonds and soccer fields are? Has a lot changed since then?"

Isis replied, *"Well, dear, as you can guess, there were many, many more trees. And animals were abundant throughout this space – there were fox and deer and other four-leggeds. The variety of the flying ones was much grander than it is today… but many lost their homes when many of my relatives lost their lives, including my dear grandmother's life. "*
I could hear the sadness in her voice.

"The swimmers – wow! My grandmother always used to say, 'You should have seen all that inhabited the waters!' Many of them are not here anymore either. The waters have become so dirty now. The swimmers could not breathe in the waters anymore. Although some found their way to other waters and some of the strongest of the swimmers adapted to the waters, there were others that were not strong enough to survive the corruption that entered the waters. I dream of the day when we can all breathe better once again, including the swimmers.
The creepers and crawlers lived here too. And even in my short lifetime I have seen some of these changes. I remember seeing a creeper that flew at

night and lit up like a flash of light for a brief moment, fly some more, and light up again. I don't see these anymore. I wonder where they have gone?" she asked.

And it dawned on me then ... "Ahhhh! You mean lightning bugs! Come to think of it... I hardly ever see lightning bugs anymore. Why is that?"
"I'm not sure, dear" she answered. *"So many things have changed, it seems, since the stories of my grandmother. So many things have changed during my life, too."*

And I added, "And during my life, too."

Then I asked her, "Why did it all have to change?"

And sadly, we both shook our heads knowing the answer, but not understanding it – and knowing we never would.

"And, then listen to what she tells you and listen to what she is saying in between the words . . . in the silence. "   ~ Kate Trnka

SINGER

"He that planteth a tree is a servant of God, he provideth a kindness for many generations, and faces that he hath not seen shall bless him."
- Henry Van Dyke

SINGER – THE SOWER

I was on my way out of the woods when I saw them – thousands and thousands of seeds scattered all over the freshly fallen snow. It was impossible not to notice them. Some of the seeds lay on the ground individually, while others had fallen from the trees in clumps. Of course I turned to look at the tree where they had come from, and thought to myself I'll be back to get that story. But, I couldn't go home just yet – the tree was urging me to get its story then – today.
It was a very brief message – so this will be a very brief story.

"I am the sower. These are my seeds – I send them out, each with their own gifts to bring to the world. People, like these seeds, are all given gifts that they are to bring to the world. Some people have a sole purpose – others have many gifts to bring. Some of my seeds will germinate right here in this park. Others will be scattered by the winds and they will land where the Creator has designed them to take root.

"And ..." she sighed, *"Some of them will begin to grow and their lives will be taken by someone who was being careless – either showing off their bravado or simply not recognizing the value of this individual tree. Still others will grow to be adult trees and then cut down because someone believed their purpose was to make paper, or help build a house or a piece of furniture. And I can only speak for myself, but I believe that some of us have such a purpose. We know that some of us will lose our lives for the purposes of man – and we don't mind as much when we know we will be appreciated. Still others of us are used to keep people warm and again what a wonderful gift to bring to someone! I only wonder how often these people **thank** the Standing People for the gifts we've provided to them.*

Things are easier for people now, so they take things for granted. By the time they get a piece of furniture in their homes they have forgotten the sacrifices it took to get that piece to where it is. All the trees!!! I guess I would just like people to know that it is important when one receives a gift – to be grateful for it. When a life is taken, to honor that life with gratitude."

I thanked Singer for his lesson and walked home.

THE MEDICINE MAN

"There is always Music amongst the trees in the Garden, but our hearts must be very quiet to hear it."

- Minnie Aumonier

THE MEDICINE MAN

I went for a walk in the woods today. My spirit needed to be out and free and in the company of those who understood, those who wouldn't judge – those who would love me unconditionally. I knew I'd find another story out there – it was time. I was excited to be able to write down another story so I could share it with others. I began to lose my footing (it was a slippery, kind of slushy day) and I found myself facing a particular tree. I thought that this was my sign to attempt to communicate with this tree. I am always humbled by my experiences in the woods. For, it was while I was visiting with this tree – trying to connect with its energy - that I heard this- one, rustling leaf. My attention kept being detracted from connecting with the particular tree I was in physical contact with to the leaf – dancing away in the wind. Dancing away – dancing away. I couldn't connect with this first tree, because that one leaf kept making noise! Dancing away – dancing away.

Well, I admit I can be a slow learner at times ... but I did finally go over to that tree with the dancing leaf, finally realizing that it was this particular tree that I was to connect with today. So, I touched the big oak and looked up at the leaf that had captured my attention. Since the leaf was dancing, I began to dance with it. It was a very energetic dance – and soon my spirit began to lift. I noticed the smile on my face. It wasn't the only thing smiling - so was my spirit. Although I was tired from my dancing, my spirit was free once again. I thanked the old oak tree.

And now, I just listened and watched that leaf – then I leaned up against the tree and closed my eyes – hearing the leaf once again. It sounded like a rattle. And I asked the tree to share its wisdom with me. And it did – but it shared its wisdom with me only in colors – first in red (the wounded) – then a yellowish/orange – (being cleansed by the fire) – then white (purity). When I got to this white phase – I recognized a new freeness – a freshness within my body. The leaf was still dancing – shaking its rattle over my head – providing me with the Medicine I needed on this particular day.

The "dance" helped to remind me not to take life so seriously. Standing underneath this tree provided me with an inner cleansing –one that allowed me to realize my strength once again. During the standing time, I opened my eyes each time I heard this soft little voice in the nearby branches – hoping to catch a glimpse of this little bird. Upon one of these openings, I saw a small woodpecker.

It was then that I recognized this tree for who he was – The Medicine Man. His rattle purifying me – driving out the self-doubt, perhaps even the self-pity I had been feeling prior to coming to the woods. And as soon as I did – I heard a woodpecker and noticed one straight in front of me – two then joined hir in nearby trees and I noticed at least 4 more off to my left. They almost seemed to be showing off and dancing, much like the little leaf that captured my attention in the first place.

I began taking some picture of Medicine Man and the Standing Brothers (I will have to meet them another day). I was on my way out of the woods when …

ADAM

"Trees are sanctuaries. Whoever knows how to speak to them, whoever knows how to listen to them, can learn the truth. They do not preach learning and precepts, they preach undeterred by particulars, the ancient law of life. "   - Hermann Hesse

ADAM

I noticed a large tree whose upper part of the trunk (one of the larger upper branches) had broken off. Although part of it was still attached to this tree, the rest of it was resting on several branches of several of the surrounding trees. Upon closer inspection, I noticed that its second main upper branch (part of the trunk) had already been lost.

It was clear to me that this tree was in transition – from a member of the Standing People to its return to Mother Earth. I stepped back to really look at it. I noticed a wise face within its bark. I took a picture of it and hope I was able to capture it. I got closer to this tree and looked up and also began to notice that within its structure I could see a body of sorts in its trunk. I could see the legs and hips, the torso – its outstretched arm and its amputated arm - its neck and head reaching toward the sky. I hope this shows up in my picture too!

Anyway, I wanted to connect with this tree as well (of course) – before it passed on and I could no longer tell its story. When I got close to it – its energy field was very strong – it was as if it almost resisted me. So I backed off – just waiting until the time was right for hir. I stepped back and just began to look - and I looked some more. Once I recognized I was welcome, I got real close to the tree awaiting hir message.
And here it is:
"*There are creatures that live here, those that you can see- those that you can hear - those you cannot see and those that you cannot hear - those you can feel and those you cannot feel… yet.*

You see my body in this tree – but I am just a physical representation of all that is.

Find peace in the stillness.

Find an awareness that wasn't there before.

You can now see things in a new way. Just as I am passing from this life into my next phase so, too, are you joining a new phase in your life. You will be able to see things in a new and different light. Your vision will be different than it ever has been before. Know that the breeze that makes our branches move, our leaves rustle and the birds soar - know that this is all connected to who we are and what we're about -that we are here to support one another.

We support your life. Remember us and support ours. What your people are doing to the environment is killing us. You are literally killing us with your saws and your bulldozers, but you're also hurting us by what you put into the air. It's hard to breathe now. The air used to be so clean and now it's so hard to breathe. Some of us are dying because we can't breathe the way we used to. It must be like those kids who have asthma – who are having breathing difficulties. It's the environment you are creating for them. They need to breathe freely – they need the air to be cleaner. There are many of you who are trying to create that again and for you we are grateful. For some of us, it is too late.

Look at all the young ones around us – they live in hope. They hope to someday grow to be straight and strong like I once was. They have lessons to teach and will have many more to teach as they grow in strength and stature. It is up to you and others like you – to help us – to help them. We're counting on you."

"And, with whom am I a speaking?" I asked.

"I am Adam."

"Thank you, Adam." And, I left the woods.

GANDAU

"If you wish your children to think deep thoughts, to know the holiest of emotions, take them to the woods and hills, and give them the freedom of the meadows; the hills purify those who walk upon them."
- Richard Jefferies

GANDAU

It still amazes me each time I go for my walk in the woods. This time I was on my way to the woods, still near the softball field when my attention was turned toward a large shaggy bark hickory tree.

So, having learned by now to pay attention to these types of things I began to approach this tree. I was soon connected to its energy and realized that I didn't have my camera. So I excused myself to retrieve it before I was further from home, making retrieving the camera a more difficult task.

Before returning to this tree, I heard a bird just chirping away and sure enough, it was right at the top of the tree I was about to connect with. I stood in the trees presence for a bit before I touched it – looking at its beauty - its shaggy surface. It was a delight to the eyes!

I touched it and then decided to get closer to it. I was leaning into it, my face and chest pressed up against the tree awaiting its message. When I did this I noticed a tingling of energy in my root chakra connecting its energy to my heart chakra. I learned that his name was Gandau, but no further message was forthcoming. Nothing – then it occurred to me that I wasn't in the woods, rather out in the open and quickly wondered 'what would people think of me?'

I laughed to myself – but then Gandau's message was clear –

"It matters not what people think of you, only that you are true to yourself."

But quickly I got the sense that I should be connecting with Gandau with my back against him, rather than facing him. As soon as I turned to oblige this feeling, there was a man approaching the area where I had been connecting with the tree. I smiled, a bit embarrassed, and said, "Good morning" to the passerby. He didn't ignore me despite what some may have done under similar circumstances!

Anyway, in the next moment two things occurred to me. One, that the idea of 'what if someone is watching me?' – was in fact exactly what was happening – even though I didn't "know" this since this person was behind me. Two, I remembered the second sense I had received just before the encounter with the man – "turn around." Had these two messages not occurred – I may have been startled or perhaps harmed in some other way by this approaching person.

So, in that moment, I realized that if I am in touch with my surroundings, if I am at one with all there is – I will have an awareness that exists on a very different level than what most of us perceive as normal.
Had Gandau given me these "messages"? Or was I so in tune with my surroundings that I intuitively did as I was being "told" to do? Is there a difference?

I believe that the hickory tree, or at least this particular hickory tree, Gandau, was a tree that was supportive and "had my back".
Very soon, Gandau's message came through (it seemed to be an extension of my previous dialogue with Adam):

"I want you to know that we support you. What you exhale, we inhale. What we exhale you inhale. You need us. We need you. Don't forsake us for ways that make things easier for you. The birds need us – they nest in us – they find refuge in us. The insects need us for homes - for food. The animals need us.

We all need each other. All of nature seems to realize this. It is only you humans that need to remember.

When you come out to join us you remember. We need people to come out to join us – to remember. Re-member yourself. You are a part of us – you need to rejoin us. Re-member yourself to us so that we can become one.

This is the only way that we will all survive. We need the water, you need the water – we all need the water. We absorb the water into our roots just as you absorb the water into the roots of your body by drinking it. We drink through the bottom and bring it up to the top – you bring it from the top down to the bottom.

We are not that different – we are opposites – yet we are so similar."

What more can I say? I hope I will always re-member who I am, so I can remember that feeling – that joy – that ecstasy!

"In the woods, we return to reason and faith. There I feel that nothing can befall me in life, — no disgrace, no calamity, (leaving me my eyes,) which nature cannot repair. Standing on the bare ground, — my head bathed by the blithe air, and uplifted into infinite space, — all mean egotism vanishes. I become a transparent eye-ball; I am nothing; I see all; the currents of the Universal Being circulate through me; I am part or particle of God."   - Ralph Waldo Emerson

MERCI

"So close is the union of creation with the Creator that it is impossible to say where one begins and the other leaves off."
- Ernest Holmes

MERCI

At first I saw this really cool tree and I thought it looked a little grumpy. And so I asked it, "Are you grumpy?" It replied, *"Well wouldn't you be if someone was always running into you? Beating up on you and stuff?"*

This tree happens to be located right next to a sledding hill, so this comes as no surprise that she was experiencing some frustration. Here's what Merci had to say:

"Strength. Remain strong. People are going to try and trip you up. Society's expectations are going to try and trip you up.

Guilt is no longer an option.

Live as if each day was your last.

Make choices that nurture your soul.

Be honest ... and truthful.

Honor and respect those that will come to you.

If you need strength you will find it within the Earth and within hir creatures and within yourself.

Never lose sight of the power that is innate within these living beings.

All that you need is within.

Stand tall – there are those who will try and knock you down – try and injure you. But it's not as if they do it intentionally and when you recognize that- that it's only a matter of ignorance- you will stand strong. And you will be there to support them and strengthen them.

Draw your roots deep within the Earth so that you can hold fast. Stand on your own two feet and guide and support those that fall away – giving them the guidance, strength and support that they need to go on – to push them back up onto the right path. They will know the path, after all we are One – we are all connected. Like Christ said, "When you help the least of these, you have helped me."

Let them know they'll be protected. Show them tenderness and compassion and, of course, mercy. Let them know peace, let them know love, let them know light. Let them know joy and laughter. But most of all just let them know."

Being in Merci's arms was like being in my mother's arms, totally surrounded by unconditional love, support, peace and contentment.

CHEYENNE

"If we could read the secret history of our enemies we should find in each man's life sorrow and suffering enough to disarm all hostility."
- Henry Wadsworth Longfellow

CHEYENNE

I was attracted to two long-needle pine trees. I was left with a small branch in order to communicate with it. You see, it would have been difficult to reach the tree without potentially damaging other growth around it. So, this sprig was given to me to connect with the tree. I felt pain, sorrow – pain from sorrow.

I asked the tree, "How come there is so few of you? This seems like the type of area that would have more trees like you."

"There were more trees like us. They are gone now. Man took them. You are to plant more trees like us. Earth Day, Arbor Day – these are ways you can help restore us – bring us back."

He was trying to draw me back to a different time and place. The birds came alive, my breathing was affected, and the brook sounded like it was rushing. I felt a pulse within the branch I was holding.

Then I heard Cheyenne say, *"The people used to use us for medicine and we were glad to give of ourselves for that purpose. The people also used to use us for shelter. They were always grateful for what they received from us –*

what we provided for them. Man took of us with no thanks, but with greed – with lust. They looked at us with lust.

Remember when you receive to give thanks. It is all that we ask. Give thanks. Always remember to give thanks."

And, I tried to remember when the last time it was that I said a prayer of thanksgiving and I sighed.

"Suburbia is where the developer bulldozes out the trees, then, names the streets after them."

\- Bill Vaughan

HARLEY

"Character is like a tree and reputation like a shadow.
The shadow is what we think of it; the tree is the real thing."
- Abraham Lincoln

HARLEY (and his siblings)

I ran across two little trees – a soft fir variety– they're sort of dwarfed amongst the large hardwood trees that surround them. They appear to be reaching and trying to find the sun. One is about 7 ft. tall and the other is 3.5-4 feet tall. They just make me laugh – they are so pure and innocent and wanting to do the right thing. *"We have so much to learn. And, we are so grateful to be around the trees that have so much wisdom and knowledge. We recognize that every day we are learning something new."* I learn that they are big brother and little sister.

Just then, a crow began to call out. The trees don't provide me with their names. But, they are so full of love and innocence and purity. They just make me smile – they're just so light!

I walked on and I ran into their sibling. This particular tree is off by itself and immediately introduces himself as *Harley*.

He is kind of an innocent rebel and tells me, *"I don't necessarily like the rules that have been imposed upon me (such as you need to stick together)."* He sits there by himself, not surrounded by any other trees like him.

"I am not a rebel in the sense that I'm naughty, but only in the sense that I want to be independent. Well, I know I can't be fully independent – nobody can, but I like to spread my wings. I like to see what my limitations are.

Look at me! I'm growing very strong and I'm over four feet tall right now and very much enjoying life. Yes, I've got a little obstacle ahead of me with this vine-like branch that is growing up over me. It actually was a fallen branch of some sort. If you wouldn't mind moving that off of me – I'd appreciate it."

So I moved it over a bit, hoping that it would allow Harley to grow tall and straight and strong. Good luck little buddy!

TREO

"The sacred tree, the sacred stone are not adored as stone or tree; they are worshipped precisely because they are hierophanies, because they show something that is no longer stone or tree but *sacred*, the *ganz andere* or 'wholly other'."
- Mircea Eliade, *Myths, Dreams and Mysteries*

TREO and the Spider

I met Treo several months ago, and although a connection was made at that time, it was not until today that the story came through to me.

Treo looks like, that at one time, it was three trees that grew into one big tree at the bottom.

Although I'm not sure - it *could* be that one tree branched out into three. It reminds me of the trinity –The Mind of God, The Spirit of God, and the Embodiment of God.

It was apparent to me early on in my encounter with Treo that this was going to be a different kind of story. I was holding Treo – touching hir – connecting with hir – when along came a spider. Well, actually it was already there, but at that moment I recognized it. And I *knew* then that the Treo's message was going to come through the spider. If the spider hadn't moved when it did I wouldn't have noticed it – it could have easily lost itself within Treo – but today, Treo had asked the spider to visually provide me with the Treo's message. And it did! And this is what I heard/saw:

"Sometimes life is a struggle – like an uphill battle. At times like these, take time to just stand still. Assess the situation. Take your time. Look around you. Listen. Feel. Take everything in. Use all of your senses. Don't ignore them.

Hold on. Feel what's around you. You may just need to change direction – change your path. You may need to take some time for yourself, but don't take too much time. Realize your path – recognize it. You will find the strength to continue your journey. Pause. Take a look at what you've accomplished. See where you've come from and journey onward – always taking time to enjoy the process.

Sometimes you'll have to go very quickly. Don't forget to nourish your body along the way. Sometimes the road will be very easy and the path will be easy to see. Find nourishment along the way for those more difficult times, because the road won't always be paved so easily. Remember to always assess the situation before you move forward- making sure you are on the right path, because things change.

Sometimes you'll have moved forward so quickly that you will not have realized which way you turned. You may find yourself backed up into a corner. Wait there. Don't rush out. Hold steadfast, because it may just be something that you're not comfortable with, or it may just be the comfort you seek and you're afraid of it. This is a time where you may feel lost from yourself – lost from the world. Sometimes being lost means being found. Blending in. Feeling whole. Being a part of everything. Having everything.

So, rest now. Find the peace in just being and existing. Find the joy in the stillness."

THE EAGLE TREE

"Because they are primeval, because they outlive us, because they are fixed, trees seem to emanate a sense of permanence. And though rooted in earth, they seem to touch the sky. For these reasons it is natural to feel we might learn wisdom from them, to haunt about them with the idea that if we could only read their silent riddle rightly we should learn some secret vital to our own lives; or even, more specifically, some secret vital to our real, our lasting and spiritual existence." - Kim Taplin, Tongues in Trees

THE EAGLE TREE

I was standing in the presence of a great one ... I asked him if he knew I was writing a book on tree stories and he said, *"Yes, and I have many great stories to tell you."*
So, I feel that this tree may have a book of its own.

*"The spirit that resides within me is a strong one.
I stand tall, I stand large, I stand proud. New trees surround me. They want to be near me, and yet they want to protect me as well.*

I don't need protection as you can see - I've stood the test of time. I have been here for many, many, many years. I have seen much. I have felt much…

Be confident in your journey - your path – the way that has been set before you.

The twists and turns that have been given to you are there for a purpose. They allow for a gentle flow through life. Although it may not seem like it at the time, if the path were straight and narrow it would rush by much too quickly - without enjoyment. The curves in the paths allow us to slow down – to take a look at life– to listen to the things that remain most important to us.

Speaking of time, find those things to that which you are drawn. When participating in those, time no longer matters. I don't know how long I've been here – just many, many, many years. But to me, time is just a measurement. I've enjoyed my life. Find the path that suits you."

How do I know which path it is? I asked.

"*You **know**! And there are no dead ends. Dead ends only exist within your mind. Keep journeying. New paths are set forth every day. The deer create them, the bunnies create them and, in the sky, the birds create them. And in the woods, we trees create them.*

Journey forth, for there is no wrong way to travel. Through each choice we learn different lessons and those lessons bring us back to our path and keep us focused on our goals. You will gain wisdom and knowledge each step of the way.

Pay attention. Stay awake. For it is through this "awakeness" – this presence- being present in the present - that you will learn what it is you are here to learn. Honor and respect all that are within your environment, within your place. For they are all a part of the wisdom that you are seeking. Enjoy!"

After talking to this spectacular tree I stepped back to get a better look at it and noticed what looked like an eye within the trees' bark. So I continued walking to see if I might see more of the face. And as I did, I noticed what looked like a beak within the bark and then the other eye. It looked, to me, like the face of an eagle. And after what happened to me on the way to work that day, I'd say the eagle energy was all around me. And what an incredibly wonderful feeling that is!

(On my way to work I decided to stop by to see if the eagles were in their nest. I'm lucky enough to live right down the street from a nest. And, I saw the young eagles, testing their wings along the rim of the nest. First one...then, the other. Just lifting themselves off the nest a few inches and landing back down on the nest again. I stayed as long as I could to watch, but then had to be off on my way.)

SCOTTY

"Trees are poems that the earth writes upon the sky."

- Kahlil Gibran

Scotty - The Young One

I met a tree very near to my house ... a young one ... Scotty. His blossoms look like little brown fuzzy things and his energy is very vibrant.

The tree reminded me of something very important. It told me:

"Do not ignore the young ones. For they have much to teach you, too. Though you are gaining in wisdom and knowledge – they have knowledge and wisdom innate within them, that you have long forgotten. They can bring this out in you.

Pay attention to them. Pay attention to what they say and what they don't say.

Pay attention to their body language because it is there that you will find the truth.

They say so much with their bodies and their faces. Some of them – their faces have learned to lie, but look beyond their faces – look to the fear in their eyes – to the tension in their bodies – then you'll know.

Look to see when your words have caused them harm by watching their bodies droop. Or when your words have strengthened them as they stand up and walk away full of pride.

Your words are very powerful to these people – these young people. They're equally as powerful to all people. But in the youth, if you pay attention, you will know the impact your words have had upon these.

Don't ignore us just because we are small. Many lessons can be learned through us and with us. You have lessons to teach us as well and we know that. But, I think that you forget that we can be teachers as well.

Life is about learning. Take this role seriously and learn from everything and everyone. Learn from the robin that chirps behind you. Learn from the crow that calls out before you. Learn from the ducks that flew into your yard just now. Learn from the ant that crawls beneath you.

Learn from every blade of grass, from every leaf on the tree."

IGLEMISUS

"I have always found thick woods a little intimidating, for they are so secret and enclosed. You may seem alone but you are not, for there are always eyes watching you. All the wildlife of the woods, the insects, birds, and animals, are well aware of your presence no matter how softly you may tread, and they follow your every move although you cannot see them."
- Thalassa Cruso

IGLEMISUS

As I approached this particular tree which had caught my eye on previous visits to the woods, I began, "I remember you. I remember your strength. I remember your wisdom. I don't remember all of your eyes. They must belong to the one who is all-seeing. Thank you for your presence here and for your presence in my life. I am writing a tree story book and one of the reasons is because of you. You got me talking to trees. May I know your name? May I have your story?"

"You are right - I do see much. I did not realize that I have eyes like those of humans, but I do see a lot. And it is because of this vision that those who seek me out - seek me out for this wisdom- the wisdom that comes with the ages. For now my name is not important. You do not know this name."

My mind was more curious than ever and, is if the tree sensed I could not let go of the whole name idea, it said,

"Your mind is trying to search for a rational answer for this name, but there is none. It is not a name that you are familiar with. I will give it to you in letters. I-G-L-E-M-I-S-U-S. *Iglemisus. That is my name. I'm really glad you came to speak with me today. I have heard of your storybook and I'm glad to be a part.*

What I have to tell you is to remember to take time - take time to enjoy life and nature. To just be - to just exist. And it is in this existing - in this experience of existing - that you will find peace and balance and harmony once again. You travel to and fro and often this is your path.

But, be still and know. Be still and know that in the stillness, lies peace. It is here that you will find the answers to the questions you are seeking. It is here you find the strength to go on - to give the gifts that have been offered to you for you to share with others.

It is in this time that you find calm assurance. That your life is worth living and that it is valuable. It is in this time that you recognize the interconnectedness of all that exists. Like the ant that crawls on the tree before you, whose presence you were aware of even before you opened your eyes. You were aware of the presence of the winged fouls who landed in the water just before you moments ago, and your interconnectedness with them. And even still, you are aware of the interconnectedness you have with the cars that travel on the bridge in the distance.

To you, at times, these cars are a nuisance, but you are connected to these as well - to that part of your life - traveling to and fro- to get you from point A to point B. It is a necessary part of your life. Do not turn away from it but don't get so caught up in it that you forget where you need to be - where you need to remember to go and to return to when everything becomes unbalanced. For it is within nature that you will find balance.

Nature will be here for you. It always has been and always will be.

Remember to be kind to nature so that we will be here for you - always. You come to me for my wisdom and for the wisdom of the other trees in these woods of this park. And we are grateful that you are open to us and receiving our messages.

Keep your heart open to the messages that are being brought to you. Share them for people need to hear them - over and over and over again.

"I frequently tramped eight or ten miles through the deepest snow

to keep an appointment with a beech-tree,

or a yellow birch, or an old acquaintance among the pines."

- Henry David Thoreau

PERSEPHONE

God is the experience of looking at a tree and saying, "Ah!" - Joseph Campbell

PERSEPHONE

I met an oak tree standing at the top of the hill of the entrance to the park, alongside the road. The leaves were just starting to branch out/bud. The tree was filled with mini oak leaves. I could see all the branches because the leaves were not full yet. It was (and still is) an outstanding display of beauty!

And here's what Persephone had to say today:

"I welcome you. I welcome you to this place. I welcome you to this path. I welcome you to this journey.

Every choice that you make – every path that you take is the right one for you in that time – in that moment.

Feel free to explore the gifts before you - the gifts that you've already received and those that you will. But remember, receiving is only a part of the equation.

Give – there are so many people that need to know.

As the bee that buzzes before you knows to continue on – to find that perfect place- to rest and to do its job… and sometimes … to just be.

A squirrel scampers next to you –foraging for its food. You too must forage – forage ahead for the gifts that are about to be given to you. Store them up and share them with the others. The others are in need too. The food of light – the food of love - the food of the Christ consciousness. The energy that you've discovered, the energy you know … people yearn for it – people want it but they don't know how to express their longing. Show them what they need. Give them what they need. Ask them to come to you and they will come. It is your duty and obligation to show them the way to love and light - to joy and to healing. It's the only way your heart really knows. Follow it.

Follow your heart, and, what you need, will follow."

ARIES

"What we are doing to the forests of the world is but a mirror reflection of what we are doing to ourselves and to one another."- Mahatma Gandhi

ARIES

"Sometimes evil finds its hands
Sometimes people make poor choices
The innocent suffer

I'm not sure what causes someone to have that hatred
That madness within themselves
That courses through their veins
To employ such horrors on someone else

It should not be this way
My only guess is that
This person felt that horrible about himself
So horrible that he knows no conscience
The things he did
The choices he made as a child were frowned upon –
Were treated with hatred
And disgust
And he knew not the tools to
As you would say, "let it slide off his back"
So he took them within himself
And it is in here that you find harm

When someone raises a hand to you
Your body is harmed but your soul is harmed far worse
And when people become evil or perform evil acts
It is because their soul has been harmed in such a way
That they need to express this hate ... this horror externally
Because they can no longer function with it internally

Ahh! But the pain and the horror
How the people who are affected ...who have been attacked
Who have been mistreated by these
It's a vicious cycle

For we all feel the impact of each decision made by another
Only when we experience what another has experienced
Do we have a full understanding of what has taken place
And how it affects us

*It's important to bring in compassion and understanding to each individual
Every time we meet someone*

*There are signs when a person isn't right
And you can feel them and you know them*

*Take time to listen
Take time to try and understand
Take time to help*

*Some of the evil may be dissipated
Before it rears its ugly head on another
And more pain exists in the world as a result*

*Be with one another
Support with one another
Listen and share and comfort one another
Most of all love one another."*

SARAH

"A tree is beautiful, but what's more, it has a right to life; like water, the sun and the stars, it is essential. Life on earth is inconceivable without trees."   - Anton Chekhov

SARAH

I found myself attracted to a tree whose bark had been inundated with new growth all up and down her trunk. It was, in essence, forming new branches. It appears as though it is being decorated with these new branches. And this is what Sarah had to say:

"I am that which gives birth to the new.
There are many phases in life - birth, growth, maturity, and rebirth
And eventually, the ending of life as we know it.
A physical death, but not a spiritual one.
Many reach a certain phase in life and choose not to continue growth.

The grounds are no longer fertile.
They think that they know the way.

I have chosen to remain open to new ideas, new thoughts...to change.

As a result, many have scoffed.
Many have met me and thought me strange.

But as you know, this also makes me that much more attractive.

It brings new things to me.

Things I would not have experienced if I hadn't been receptive to them.
It is my hope – it is my passion in life – to give this message to those who are willing to hear it.

Remain open to change – to growth – to new possibilities – each and every day.

For each opportunity that presents itself – is an opportunity for a new way to express love in this world.

To express ourselves – the inner core of who we are.

Choose love – which is ONEness with all that is.

Be strong even when others try to make you weak.

Be open to the new possibilities and growth.

In this you will find freedom and renewal."

ARTHUR

"Trees are the earth's endless effort
to speak to the listening heaven."
- Rabindranath Tagor

ARTHUR

"This story is about new beginnings – the end of something old – the beginning of something new.

My name is Arthur.

I've asked the furry one's to remove themselves from most of me so that you could contact me.
(There were furry little caterpillars climbing all over Arthur!)

You ask why they're here and I really don't know. But, I've grown attached to them. And obviously, they're attached to me!"

"I have been standing here a long time waiting for you. Waiting for you to share my message with the people of this Earth – of this day and age.

Things used to be so different. I knew this day would come – when people have forgotten the ways – forgotten the way of respect –forgotten the way of love.

I stand tall and strong like many of the trees that are around. They seem to evoke a sense of transition and that is the message I bring to you today. It is time for the world to transit – to move from what we are now to what is to be.

Long ago the people of this Earth knew what it was to love and respect all that is – to honor. There is very little honor today. I know that there are people – pockets of people that are remembering. Re-membering ... what it is to feel again – what it is to know. To truly understand. To look at the meaning behind things. Not to ignore – not to drive so fast that we don't fully comprehend the magnitude – the sacredness of life.

Transition – people go through many of these in their life. Then, ignore the most important transition of all – coming back to self. Coming back to the awareness of the sacredness of life.

Making decisions that honor that sacredness, not only to themselves, but to others. When you go home, I want you to study the word transition. I will speak to you again. I will give you further the message that is required of you to give to those for whom you are writing this. In the meantime, go in peace and wisdom and honor."

AUDREY

"Among archetypal images, the Sacred Tree is one of the most widely know symbols on Earth. There are few cultures in which the Sacred Tree does not figure: as an image of the cosmos, as a dwelling place of gods or spirits, as a medium of prophecy and knowledge, and as an agent of metamorphoses when the tree is transformed into human or divine form or when It bears a divine or human image as its fruit or flowers."
 - Christopher and Tricia McDowell, *The Sanctuary Garden*

AUDREY

"It's nearing the end of the season. Many chapters are closing and new one's beginning. Take the time and close those chapters, so that you can move on and reap the benefits of what is to come.

I spread a path of leaves before you so you may walk softly. The journey will be an easy one in many, many ways because you are not resisting it. Because you want to see it – because you know – you know that to fight it is fruitless.

Watch and listen to the ebb and flow of all that is. During the ebb, sit still and wait. You can struggle against it, but don't waste your energy in that way. So that when it is time to flow, you'll have everything you need to take you even further down your path.

So many people leave things undone. And this draws upon their energy - day in and day out. A lot of times they don't even recognize it. I want you to recognize those things that are left undone and take care of them. Put them to rest. Your energy will be needed ahead of you. And if you can invest fully yourself into what lies ahead, you will be amazed at the results. People who enter your life to help you along the way, to find that which you were seeking, be open to it, trust it, believe in it, know it. It is with this conviction, and this understanding of things that you will succeed.

Go with the rhythm of nature; go with the rhythm of the universe. Go with the rhythm of your heart and soul. You can't go wrong. Now go."

ABIGAIL

"We have nothing to fear and a great deal to learn from trees, that vigorous and pacific tribe which without stint produces strengthening essences for us, soothing balms, and in whose gracious company we spend so many cool, silent and intimate hours."
- Marcel Proust, *Pleasures and Regrets*

ABIGAIL

I was called to sit against a tree today. It called to me – asked me to come over. I've been troubled with some sore muscles in my back from overextending myself. It asked me to lean up against it and be healed. Here is the message I received:

"You can be one with all that is. It seems that for people like you – people of the day... In order to do that sometimes you just need to be still.

Reconnect.

But, you can do this. Draw yourself in, draw yourself closer and you will feel the connection, the web, the Oneness, the wholeness and it is here you will find peace. The peace that everyone is seeking – inner peace.
Those that have crossed over know this peace because they are back. They are a part of the embodiment of all that is. They long to share that wholeness with you.

They lead you in ways to try and capture this feeling of utter joy. Where you make your mistake is that you ignore these signs - the signs that send you one way or another on your journey.

That inner voice which you call your Higher Self or your conscience – this is what is already connected to the whole. And when you choose to ignore it you break yourself from it.

You are going to want to decide to listen to this voice, this inner voice, this inner self. And when you do, your choice will be great. You will find happiness in your decisions. You will find peace with all that is. Learning to trust it is the hardest thing. It is the hardest lesson.

But I tell you, that as you begin to trust and listen, listen and trust – each and every step along the way will be an easier one. Even when you find sorrow, you will again feel joy because you have an understanding of the whole. So as you go back into the world as you know it, find time for stillness. Find time for wholeness. Find time for all that is."

JEREMY

"We shall be made truly wise if we be made content, not only with what we can understand, but content with what we do not understand…"   - Charles Kingsley

JEREMY

Today I met Jeremy and Geronimo. They are twins. They are large and they grow tall and proud.

I'm talking with Jeremy right now; I need to rethink the gender of the other tree. For some reason it feels very feminine. Anyway...
Jeremy's presence is astoundingly powerful. He said,

"I have much to tell you. Much you need to know. It comes from the wisdom of the ages. It comes from the grandfathers that surround me that you've taken notice of today for the very first time. They speak to you of truth, of love, of peace, of sorrow, of frustration and anger at times. Within the grandfathers are all of these emotions and yet, they are at peace with them.

It is important that you know and recognize that all emotion is okay. It is a part of the experience. It is a part of what is. Feel free to express those emotions but be sure they are in healthy forms, in healthy ways as I know you will. But, don't be afraid of them. Experience them, and in this you will find what true life is all about. You will experience the fullness of life as it was meant to be lived.

Don't ignore the feelings when they surface, but go with them. Understand them. Know them. Appreciate them. May you know the pain of disappointment, of pain, of sorrow and the joy and the pure ecstasy of love and truth.

There are many other emotions that surface within life. Embrace those as well. Embrace them fully. And when you do, true wisdom will come to you. True wisdom will embrace you. Show others how to experience these things in a healthy way. It is your task to help them to experience this. But first, you must do it yourself. I have many more things to teach you, to share with you. I have lived a very full life and have seen many things. I will be here for a long time still. I am strong. But it is because of what I have experienced that I have this strength and this wisdom. Open yourself up to life fully so that you can have it too."

GERONIMO (with Jeremy)

"The first peace, which is the most important, is that which comes within the souls of people when they realize their relationship, their oneness, with the universe and all its powers, and when they realize at the center of the universe dwells the Great Spirit, and that this center is really everywhere, it is within each of us." – Black Elk

GERONIMO

I stepped in front of Jeremy's twin and began to feel something I've felt only a couple of times in my life. It was one of those times when my emotions were full and immediately at the surface. And this is what I heard:

"You are experiencing something that Jeremy just talked about – pure love. Pure understanding. Pure connection. It's all so beautiful, isn't it? It's the most glorious thing! It is a connection that is beyond knowing. It's beyond words, beyond experience. You have to be open to it though, it won't come to you unless you are. And you are so open right now. We are all open to receiving you and to giving to you.

This interchange is so important – this exchange of energy that needs to exist. It needs to exist amongst everything – every single thing.

Give freely that you will receive freely.

Know this – if I can teach you nothing else – know this: Give. Keep giving. You will receive more than you can ever imagine. But, don't give with attachment. Give with love - give with freedom. Give from the heart and the soul.

There are so many ways to give. Your time. Your energy. Your laughter. Your silence. Your passion. Your heart. Your love. Your tears. You can even give with your pain – not to give pain, not to inflict pain. As Jeremy said all these emotions are gifts – gifts to you, to your soul – gifts to the Universe. When others see you experiencing them and feel you experiencing them – we are all at one. This is what I want you to know – this is what we want you to know."

LIBERTY

"When you enter a grove peopled with ancient trees, higher than the ordinary, and shutting out the sky with their thickly inter-twined branches, do not the stately shadows of the wood, the stillness of the place, and the awful gloom of this doomed cavern then strike you with the presence of a deity?"

- Seneca

LIBERTY

"If you want love you have to give it unconditionally. What you give - you will receive. It is unconditional love that you would like to feel. Everyone would. It's what we all want – it's what we all desire. When people look at your life I hope they know that you live within your heart – within your soul. Within the spirit and the compassion and the mercy that exists when you know what unconditional love is and that you're able to give it freely, even when others can't give it back to you, because that's not freedom.

If you give only when it's easy – only when you know you will receive - it is no longer unconditional. You must learn to give and give and give. You will find the strength when you need it. You always have - otherwise you wouldn't be here. You wouldn't be listening to this message. So, you know it within your heart that you can face any challenges and obstacles that come your way. As long as you lead with the love in your heart – the love that brings you such joy, such ecstasy. It is this gift that you bring to the world which matches no other.

The gifts you bring – this gift of love will come back to you in ways you never dreamed possible. It is in this love that you find freedom, true peace and understanding

Come back to us if you need the strength to carry on. We are here for you - just as you are here for us."

PAZ

"I never saw a discontented tree. They grip the ground as though they liked it, and though fast rooted they travel about as far as we do. They go wandering forth in all directions with every wind, going and coming like ourselves, traveling with us around the sun two million miles a day, and through space heaven knows how fast and far!"   - John Muir

PAZ

"Hear me now. I am at peace within my soul because I am following my true path. I choose to live in harmony with all that is contained within the Universe. I live in truth. I live in love. In knowing this – this is where I find my peace. Many of you have caught glimpses of this type of peace and then you forgot.

You forget because you don't live in the true love… in the truth.

Try to remain steadfast in this love and in this truth so that you might attain the peace that comes with understanding.

This is true wisdom."

THE ANGEL TREE

"A few minutes ago every tree was excited, bowing to the roaring storm, waving, swirling, tossing their branches in glorious enthusiasm like worship. But though to the outer ear these trees are now silent, their songs never cease. Every hidden cell is throbbing with music and life, every fiber thrilling like harp strings, while incense is ever flowing from the balsam bells and leaves. No wonder the hills and groves were God's first temples, and the more they are cut down and hewn into cathedrals and churches, the farther off and dimmer seems the Lord himself."   - John Muir

THE ANGEL TREE

I saw a tree and was on my way down to her when my foot got caught up in a small animal hole in the ground. This tree has been scarred, from what I do not know, but in this is her beauty. Here is what she told me:

"Others may try and trip you up. It is best not to resist the fall. When you try and resist the fall that is when you crash.

But, if, as you are tripped – you allow that feeling to take place – if you let your body fall into the helplessness, your body reacts. It finds a way. It finds a way to maintain that balance. It finds a way to keep you upright, to keep you on your path.
 It is the fear of falling that will make you do so. It is the knowing that in the stumbling you can gain strength through the process, if you just go with it and believe in it.

Believe that everything will be okay. Sure at first there is this instant panic. A questioning of 'How did that happen?' Where did this come from? And often it is problems that blind-side us – we don't see them coming. But again, it is how we choose to react to that problem, that situation, that thing that tries to trip us up.

We can choose fear and fall, or we can choose faith and fly. The choice is yours. What will you do?"

"We can choose fear and fall,

or, we can choose faith and fly."

-Kate Trnka (via the Angel Tree)

HARLEY (AGAIN)

"Evolution did not intend trees to grow singly. Far more than ourselves they are social creatures, and no more natural as isolated specimens than man is as a marooned sailor or hermit." - John Fowles

HARLEY

I wasn't expecting this, but Harley is bringing me another message. The little one reminds us that we need to rely on each other from time to time for our growth and well-being and to help us to manage our lives when we are in a vulnerable place.

Harley says, *"Don't become entangled in having to be strong. Sometimes strength is found in asking for help, recognizing your vulnerabilities, recognizing your weaknesses, recognizing that you have no control over the situation. And in order to get past your vulnerabilities you need to find strength and sometimes that strength cannot come from within but needs to be gathered and harvested from those around you, who choose to support your life, and, who choose to support your dreams.*

My dream is to survive in this place. I chose this spot which is a very difficult one in which to grow. I wonder if these vines recognize the strength within me and are trying to suffocate me and pull that out of me so that I don't survive. But I have found that the right person will come along to assist me on my path – my journey. The right situation will present itself in the right time. And in that situation, you will be relieved from the burden - that absolute burden that almost crushed the life right out of you. That person will meet with you, with love and trust and understanding and give it to you without harming themselves, without harming you, without harming others. They will find a way to help you on your journey.

But, you must first decide what your journey is. What is your destination? What does it look like? What does it feel like? When you can live within that feeling – when you can really feel it ... you know ... that aliveness that comes from that dream, from that passion, from that desire that burns inside of you – the one that lets you know that you are on the right path! When you can live within that feeling – that's where you'll find your strength. And sometimes you're going to need a hand up, like I did today.

But it is in that vulnerability and in that weakness that true love and relationship develops with another being. Many do not have this understanding – many have not learned this lesson, but it is an awesome one. One that you can take with you and fly with."

ROSE

"If trees could scream, would we be so cavalier about cutting them down? We might, if they screamed all the time, for no good reason."
- Jack Handey

ROSE

"I'm glad you came to me today because you never really did get to know me. That's the way it's been with my life - nobody taking the time to get to know me. I've been injured. I have pain. It is not dissimilar to the pain you experience when you have a loss. A part of your soul removed carelessly. Sometimes one hurt causes another. One seeming loss - one seeming misunderstanding, one seeming act of carelessness can have a ripple effect. But in my case, the careless tragedy was met in a place that hurt me greatly, but not so much that I'm not able to survive. The loss of a part of me, and the injury that it caused another part of me, will always remain - lost and injured.

But what I want you to know now is that I have a choice. I have a choice to continue grieving my loss and my pain and living within that pain. Or, healing the pain - allowing it some time to subside and continue growing upward - reaching for the sky, reaching for the stars, reaching for the sunshine.

And although I still live in some of the pain, because it's still so real - I know in time and through my healing process that the pain will subside. That the loss will be a distant memory, and that my life will continue to grow and prosper. I know this because it is my choice and it is what I must do. It is life. And, so it is with all of life."

Bella, Bertha and Rose – The Three Sisters

Scars of Bella

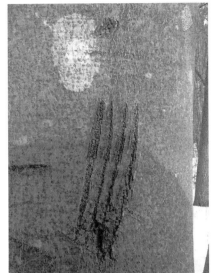

Scars of Bertha

EDWARD

"The best friend on earth of man is the tree: when we use the tree respectfully and economically we have one of the greatest resources of the earth."

- Frank Lloyd Wright

Although I met Edward much earlier on in my journey through the woods, his words didn't come to me until now...the very last story of this book...

"I dare. I dare you. I dare you to dream. I dare you to dream those dreams. Those dreams give us hope...and inspiration. The dreams are the breath of life.

The people that used to live here had dreams.

Breathe in life. Dance in the wind. Sing. And play!

I dare you!

Listen to the sounds of your soul and sing them out! Rejoice!

Let those dreams rustle within your soul so that others might hear that rustling and be inspired...so that YOU might be inspired.

It is time. It is time to break out of the fear and the procrastination and the self-doubt and trust. Trust that your life has purpose and meaning. And, it is your time to go forth and pursue this.

Pursue this dream that you've long held on to...for whatever reason. The work that you are doing within your own self and within your own soul is helping you to release these embedded patterns of stagnation and you are opening up your life, and your heart, and your soul to its purpose.

Your soul purpose is what we call "dreams". I dare you. I dare you to pursue that dream. I dare you to pursue that dream today. Now. Right now."

Epilogue

Through my journey of walking through the woods, and developing my relationship with the Standing People, I have learned that their lives present themselves to me not only in their time, but in my time as well. However, I am only open to receiving their message when I am in the place to do so. I believe everything in our lives teach us lessons. When we are open to receiving them, it is only then that we will be given those messages – those life lessons, that are so profound - if we only listen and take the time to discover and to experience within the present moment… For that is all we have…the gift of NOW – a present – THE present.

I believe that the Standing People are here to support us. I know that they have supported me and I hope that through their stories, they will support you along your journey. There are many more tree stories to share with you and I intend to spend my life doing just that. This book has finally been completed and will be sent to the printer today. The next one begins tomorrow!

I am blessed.

Thank you for taking the time to read my personal experiences and allowing me to share these stories with you.

May you know peace. May you know truth. And most of all, may you know love.

And, may you know the stories of the trees in *your* life. They are there to answer you, to guide you, to teach you and to love you.

"When I would recreate myself, I seek the darkest wood, the thickest and most interminable, and to the citizen, most dismal swamp. I enter a swamp as a sacred place - a sanctum sanctorum. There is the strength, the marrow of nature. The wild-wood covers the virgin mould - and the same soil is good for men and trees."

- Henry David Thoreau